Progress (G)
Trackers (G)

3–5 years

by
Dr Hannah Mortimer

A QEd Publication

Published in 2004

© Hannah Mortimer

ISBN 1 898873 35 6

British Library Cataloguing
A catalogue record for this book is available from the British Library.

Published by QEd, The ROM Building, Eastern Avenue, Lichfield, Staffs. WS13 6RN
Web site: www.qed.uk.com
Email: orders@qed.uk.com

Printed in the United Kingdom by Stowes (Stoke-on-Trent).

Contents

Guidance for parents

In early years settings there is a requirement that staff observe and record what children do. These observations should then be used to help plan the next steps of children's play, learning and development. With this in mind *Trackers 3-5* (and the earlier *Trackers 0-3*) were developed to provide a simple method of meeting this requirement.

The Trackers link into the Government's *Curriculum guidance for the foundation stage* (QCA, 2000). This relates to children aged three to six years. The Trackers are divided into various types of play activity and the six areas of learning.

Within each area of learning, the Government has identified Early Learning Goals (G) which most children will be expected to have achieved by the end of their Reception year. Each of these goals is divided into smaller sections called Stepping Stones *,* .

The early years setting your child is attending will use a simple recording system and will share your child's progress with you. There is a section at the back of the book, and at the bottom of each page, where you can add any comments you wish to make.

Trackers 3-5 is not a definitive guide to your child's progress. This is simply one way of observing and recording progress. The rate at which Early Learning Goals are 'ticked off' may not necessarily relate directly to your child's developmental progress. It may be that staff have had more or less opportunity to observe and record certain areas of learning. It is important, therefore, not to become anxious about a recording system such as this. All children develop at different rates and this is quite normal. However, if you are concerned about your child's progress, discuss this with the relevant member of staff. If there are any significant developmental delays, this method of observation and recording will assist staff in identifying such problems so that appropriate action can be taken.

Guidance for early years staff

Who the Trackers are for
These progress trackers will be useful for early years educators working in all kinds of early years settings: nursery classes, reception classes, pre-schools, private nurseries, day nurseries and creches. It will also be helpful for individuals training on NVQ or pre-school diploma courses and of interest to childminders, parents and carers of children who are interested in tracking their children's development over the years from three to five.

The six Areas of Learning
These Trackers have been designed to be simple and usable, yet to link into the Government's *Curriculum guidance for the foundation stage* (QCA, 2000). The guidance focuses on how children learn and what adults can do to encourage that learning. It identifies six Areas of early learning:

- Personal, social and emotional development.

- Communication, language and literacy.

- Mathematical development.

- Knowledge and understanding of the world.

- Physical development.

- Creative development.

In these Trackers, each area is also divided into various types of play activity and these are reflected in the title page of each Tracker.

Why track progress?
Full day care. National Standards for under 8s day care and childminding (DfES, 2003) state that the registered person should meet children's individual needs and promote their welfare. This will involve planning and providing activities and play opportunities to

develop children's emotional, physical, social and intellectual capabilities (Standard 3). The registered person and staff are expected to observe and record what children do and use their observations to plan the next steps for the children's play, learning and development. This is a requirement of Ofsted inspection. You are also expected to be aware that some children may have special educational needs (SEN) and that you can take action to identify and meet these needs. You will be in a better position to do this if you have been able to observe and track the progress that any child is making.

One of the first checklists to adopt this play-centred approach was the *Playladders* checklist (Mortimer, 2000) though these tend to start with the competencies of children of around 18 months old and do not correspond to the six Areas of Learning. The present Trackers aim to serve as a bridge between the former methods and the new, providing confidence to workers that they can indeed track progress in a more holistic way. It is hoped that staff will use them flexibly and use them in conjunction with the *Curriculum guidance for the foundation stage* which explains in greater detail how to focus in on each Area of Learning.

Early Learning Goals
Within each Area of Learning, there are early learning goals which most children will be expected to reach by the end of their Reception year, and Stepping Stones along the way to those goals. Each page of the Trackers carries the title of one type of play activity within that particular Area of Learning, yet weaves in some of the developmental and skills-based stages which users will already be familiar with and also builds in approximations to the Stepping Stones and Early Learning Goals given in the guidance.

The Stepping Stones
Early years educators have asked us to develop progress trackers which cover years three to five and which also overlap with the QCA Early Learning Goals and Stepping Stones for development. You will

see footstep icons which tell you that certain of the statements relate closely to the foundation stage Stepping Stones. There are also Stepping Stones in *Trackers 0–3*, so you will be able to carry forward information from there to your records for three to five year-olds.

Each tracker contains about 14 statements of skills, understanding or competence, most of which can be easily observed or easily interpreted using the curriculum guidance. Some of these are taken from typical developmental stages that children pass through in their early years. Others relate to the Stepping Stones for early development or Early Learning Goals given in the QCA *Curriculum guidance for the foundation stage*. So that you can identify them easily, approximations to the Stepping Stones are marked with this sign ⸴ and the Early Learning Goals are marked with this sign Ⓖ You will find it easier to decide whether what you are observing meets the Stepping Stone or Early Learning Goal if you refer to the curriculum guidance document which has examples of children's play and learning behaviour at each of the stages. Sometimes the wording used in these progress trackers is slightly simplified from the actual Stepping Stones or goals, but again referring to the full document will make sure your own assessment fits with the QCA guidelines.

How to use the Trackers
Use one progress tracker booklet for each child. Observe the child during your daily play and care activities. If you feel that the child has reached that particular stage most of the time (we all have good days and bad days), then record the date of your observation in the column. Revisit the trackers at regular intervals. You will then find that you are gradually able to observe and record more and more skills as the child develops and gathers experiences.

Other settings prefer to adapt the recording column flexibly to suit their own recording system. For example, observations during each term are entered in a different colour with a single tick to indicate that the child sometimes manages that skill and double tick to indicate that the child has definitely mastered that skill and can demonstrate it in different situations. In other words, choose a system to suit your setting and keep it simple.

		✓	Date
Knows what the rules and boundaries are	🐾		
Works in a group	Ⓖ		
Initiates interactions with others	🐾	✓	1/03/05
Forms good relationships with adults and peers	Ⓖ	✓✓	7/03/05

There is a space at the bottom for your additional comments if they are relevant. For example, you might wish to record that a child was poorly for a while in order to explain why there was a setback in their confidence. You might add a comment that a child went into hospital for grommets on a certain date and that might explain why speech and understanding suddenly improved. You might want to use the trackers more flexibly and add qualifying comments such as 'only if a familiar adult is present'.

Make sure that you have actual evidence for each of the items you record. Work on your actual observations rather than on hearsay. This is simply because you need to know which items still need encouragement or teaching and which are well established as part of the child's repertoire.

Planning the observations
Some settings find it easiest to delegate responsibility for the tracking to different members of staff. For example, each child could be assigned to one key worker who would be responsible for tracking the development of a small group of children. Other settings might ascribe a certain Area of Learning to a particular member of staff who would also have the responsibility for planning and developing opportunities and activities in that area for that term.

Plan certain activities or opportunities which are going to allow you to observe a particular aspect of all the children's development that

session, for example sand play.
Make all observations in as natural a way as possible so that the children are not aware of a different situation or the fact that you are 'assessing' them.

Build in regular opportunities for observing as part of your regular short-term, medium-term and long-term planning.

Find regular opportunities to share progress with parents and carers. Compare notes and share successes.

Meeting individual needs
As part of your regular observing, you may notice that a particular child is developing rather patchily. Perhaps there is one or more aspect of their development that is not progressing as fast as the others. This provides you with useful information for planning new learning opportunities for that child. Because the progress trackers make you aware of the possible 'next steps' that each child passes through, you can play alongside the child to teach and encourage that step. The Trackers are not set out rigorously in developmental sequence and each child will develop individually. However, there is an approximate progression from age three to five with the youngest stages at the top of each page to the oldest stage at the bottom. You might find it helpful to track back to *Trackers 0–3* for children still at earlier stages of their development and learning.

Sometimes you might be aware that a child has SEN because their development is significantly behind what you would normally expect for that age. You will also need to refer to *The Special Educational Needs Code of Practice* (DfES, 2001) for further guidance on meeting their needs or refer to *The SEN Code of Practice in Early Years Settings* published by QEd Publications.

It is important that you *communicate* with parents regarding the progress trackers. Parents may be alarmed if they see that a large number of statements have not been 'ticked off' and may fear that their child is not progressing. These Trackers should not be seen as a definitive guide to a child's progress, they simply represent one further way of observing and recording progress. Sometimes parents may need reassuring that it is quite normal for children's development to progress at very different rates.

References

DfES (2001) *The Special Educational Needs Code of Practice.* Nottingham: DfES Publications.

DfES (2003) *Full day care. National standards for under 8s day care and childminding.* Nottingham: DfES Publications.

Mortimer, H. (2000) *Playladders.* Lichfield: QEd Publications.

Mortimer, H. (2002) *The SEN Code of Practice in Early Years Settings.* Lichfield: QEd Publications.

Qualifications and Curriculum Authority (QCA) (2000) *Curriculum guidance for the foundation stage.* Hayes: QCA Publications.

Area of Learning

Personal, social and emotional development

Trackers 3–5

Area of Learning	Personal, social and emotional development
Play activity	All about me

		✓	Date
Familiar with the group's routines	👣		
Makes connections between their play and their experiences (e.g. 'This is how Mum does it at home')	👣		
Talks about self and own experiences	👣		
Can cope with changes of routine			
Talks about own family and home	👣		
Uses words to ask for what they need	👣		
Responds to experiences with a range of feelings (e.g. happiness, anger, distress, excitement)	Ⓖ		
Uses words to express feelings (e.g. 'I'm sad')	👣		
Feels positively about themselves	👣		
Continues to be interested, excited and motivated to learn	Ⓖ		
Shows confidence and able to stand up for their rights	👣		
Understands that there are different cultures and beliefs and accepts this	Ⓖ		
Is confident to try new activities, initiate ideas and speak in a familiar group	Ⓖ		
Understands they can expect others to treat them with respect	Ⓖ		

Comments

Trackers 3–5

Area of Learning	Personal, social and emotional development
Play activity	Getting on

		✓	Date
Adapts behaviour to different occasions	👣		
Begins to share with others with support	👣		
Shows care and concern for others	👣		
Begins to make friendships			
Interested in exploring the foods and clothing of other cultures	👣		
Begins to show self-control	👣		
Knows what the rules and boundaries are	👣		
Works in a group	Ⓖ		
Initiates interactions with others	👣		
Forms good relationships with adults and peers	Ⓖ		
Understands the need for behaviour rules	Ⓖ		
Takes turns and shares fairly	Ⓖ		
Has a developing respect for their own and others' cultures and beliefs	Ⓖ		
Understands what is right/wrong and why	Ⓖ		
Considers the consequences for others of what they do (e.g. 'If I snatch this toy my friend will be upset')	Ⓖ		
Understands that people have different needs and respects this (e.g. why I should be quiet/gentle)	Ⓖ		

Comments

Trackers   3–5

Area of Learning	Personal, social and emotional development
Play activity	Toys and playthings

	✓	Date
Can share a toy with occasional adult support		
Chooses own activity to do next 👣		
Combines toys together in play (e.g. bricks and cars)		
Has favourite toys		
Actively involves others in play		
Asks permission to play with a toy		
Concentrates on an activity for over 20 minutes 👣		
Helps to tidy up and put away		
Regularly plays with more challenging toys		
Takes risks and explores within the setting 👣		
Shows another child ways of playing with a toy		
Tidies up a familiar area independently		
Plays for five minutes independently		
Maintains attention, concentrates and sits quietly when appropriate Ⓖ		

Comments

Trackers 3–5

Area of Learning	Personal, social and emotional development
Play activity	Independence

	✓	Date
Begins to understand the need to stay healthy and clean		
Uses a knife and fork when food is cut up		
Drinks from a full open cup		
Takes self to toilet and washes hands		
Finds own equipment		
Plays happily without support		
Uses rubbish bins appropriately		
Asks for help and guidance with confidence		
Pours drinks out		
Undresses independently (G)		
Manages own coat independently		
Passes around snacks		
Dresses independently (G)		
Manages own personal hygiene (G)		
Selects play activities independently and finds what is needed to enjoy that activity (G)		

Comments

Area of Learning

Communication, language and literacy

Trackers   3–5

Area of Learning	Communication, language and literacy
Play activity	Interaction

		✓	Date
Confident enough to ask for something	👣		
Talks about things they have found interesting	👣		
Shows an interest in others' conversations			
Uses actions more than talk to demonstrate to others	👣		
Talks alongside others rather than with them	👣		
Talks to adults to get their attention	👣		
Uses other children's names when speaking to them			
Is aware of the listener's point of view	👣		
Initiates a conversation	👣		
Uses talk to resolve disagreements	👣		
Turn-takes in a conversation	👣		
Talks with confidence to visitors	👣		
Interacts with others, making plans and activities and taking turns in conversation	(G)		

Comments

Trackers 3–5

Area of Learning	Communication, language and literacy
Play activity	Speaking

		✓	Date
Asks why things happen	👣		
Uses familiar phrases (e.g. 'once upon a time ...')	👣		
Begins to use more complex sentences (e.g. 'I can't because Jason's got it')	👣		
Sticks to the point most of the time	👣		
Uses simple grammatical structures (e.g. plurals, negatives, questions)	👣		
Asks simple 'where' questions	👣		
Asks simple 'what' questions	👣		
Uses words, tones and phrases from familiar books	👣		
Uses greetings, 'please' and 'thank you' regularly	Ⓖ		
Shows an awareness of the listener (e.g. pauses to make sure you are listening)	Ⓖ		
Speaks clearly and audibly with confidence and control	Ⓖ		
Extends vocabulary, exploring the sounds of new words	Ⓖ		
Makes up own stories, songs and rhymes	Ⓖ		

Comments

Trackers   3–5

Area of Learning	Communication, language and literacy
Play activity	Understanding

	✓	Date
Points to eight body parts when asked (e.g. nose, head etc.)		
Answers simple 'who' questions		
Can identify 'high'/'low' (e.g. points to the correct tower when you build two towers and ask 'which is the high/low one?')		
Answers simple 'what' questions		
Points to the 'full'/'empty' one		
Understands what to do next when you tell them		
Follows simple direction words such as in/on/under		
Identifies actions (e.g. 'Which one is sleeping?')		
Answers questions about people or events not actually present		
Understands when you talk about the future		
Joins in a discussion with comments		
Answers questions about a story		
Extends their vocabulary, exploring the meaning of new words (G)		

Comments

Trackers   3–5

Area of Learning	Communication, language and literacy
Play activity	Thinking

		✓	Date
Talks about the past	👣		
Gives a very simple explanation	👣		
Uses a wide range of words to express or elaborate ideas	👣		
Gives a running commentary as they play	👣		
Predicts what happens next	👣		
Uses talk to describe a sequence of events	👣		
Uses talk to link cause with effect (e.g. can explain why something happened)	👣		
Uses talk to pretend and imagine	👣		
Uses language for an increasing range of purposes (e.g. to ask for information, to describe, to remember and to explain)	👣		
Develops a simple story	(G)		
Talks about feelings	(G)		
Uses language to tell you what happened to them in the past	(G)		
Uses language in role play	(G)		
Uses language to imagine	(G)		
Uses talk to organise, sequence and clarify thinking/ideas	(G)		

Comments

Trackers   3–5

Area of Learning	Communication, language and literacy
Play activity	Listening

		✓	Date
Enjoys listening to nursery rhymes			
Can clap the rhythm of their name	👣		
Can tell you the sound their name begins with	👣		
Can listen to and carry out a simple direction one-to-one			
Looks at you when you begin to speak			
Can listen to some letter sounds and point to the correct letter	👣		
Can respond if the whole group is given an instruction (e.g. 'Please stop now')			
Repeats the first sound of a word (e.g. car starts with 'c')	👣		
Can continue a rhyming string (e.g. when I was one I ate a ...)	👣		
Will listen to a story for 10–15 minutes			
Enjoys listening to spoken language and can learn something new from what is said (e.g. 'I didn't know there were pink birds')	Ⓖ		
Sustains active listening, adding relevant questions, comments and actions during discussion time	Ⓖ		
Listens with enjoyment and responds to stories, songs and rhymes	Ⓖ		

Comments

Trackers 3–5

Area of Learning	Communication, language and literacy
Play activity	Picture books and early reading

		✓	Date
Recognises some familiar words (e.g. 'Mum' and their own name) when reading	🐾		
Knows that books and computers tell you things	🐾		
Selects own book and holds it correctly			
Has a favourite book and can tell you why			
Makes up words and sounds to go with their play	(G)		
Retells a simple story	(G)		
Reads simple words or sentences	(G)		
Knows that print carries meaning and goes from left to right and top to bottom	(G)		
Can tell you the sound a word begins with when listening to simple words (e.g. dog)	(G)		
Can tell you the sound a word ends with when listening to simple words (e.g. tap)	(G)		
Can repeat the short vowel sound in a word when listening to simple words (e.g. cat)	(G)		
Can name letters 'A' 'B' 'C' etc.	(G)		
Can give you the sounds of letters	(G)		
Shows an understanding of the elements of stories – can tell you what happened at the beginning, middle and end	(G)		
Uses non-fiction books to find out information	(G)		

Comments

Trackers 3–5

Area of Learning	Communication, language and literacy
Play activity	Early writing

		✓	Date
Makes marks and calls it 'writing'	👣		
Uses marks (pretend writing) to *mean* something	👣		
Draws lines and circles	👣		
Traces over letter forms	👣		
Writes a few recognisable letters	👣		
Speaks slowly enough for an adult to write it down	👣		
Tries writing a message	👣		
Writes own first name	👣		
Holds pencil correctly	👣		
Uses writing for different functions (e.g. stories, messages and lists)	Ⓖ		
Forms many letters correctly	Ⓖ		
Begins to write simple sentences	Ⓖ		
Enjoys using written language in their play	Ⓖ		
Makes a good attempt at writing a new word	Ⓖ		
Uses knowledge of letter sounds to write a few simple, regular words (e.g. c – a – t)	Ⓖ		

Comments

Area of Learning

Mathematical development

Trackers 3–5

Area of Learning	Mathematical development
Play activity	What next?

	✓	Date
Predicts what number comes next in a familiar number rhyme (e.g. 'One, two, buckle my shoe ...')		
Shows an interest in number problems		
Finds an item from directional/positional clues (e.g. 'It's in/on/under the cupboard')		
Describes a simple journey		
Orders two objects by height		
Orders three objects by length		
Orders three objects by weight/capacity		
Shows an awareness of symmetry (e.g. can make patterns on butterfly wings which are mirror images)		
Operates a remote control toy		
Uses everyday words to describe position (e.g. in/on/behind/in front of)	Ⓖ	
Talks about shapes and arrangements using words like 'circle', 'in a row', 'stripey')		
Begins to use the vocabulary involved in adding and subtracting such as 'more', 'less', 'take away'	Ⓖ	
Knows that 'adding' means combining groups together	Ⓖ	
Knows that 'subtraction' is to do with taking away	Ⓖ	
Finds one more/less than a number from 1 to 10	Ⓖ	

Comments

Trackers   3–5

Area of Learning	Mathematical development
Play activity	Sorting and matching

	✓	Date
Tells you which set of objects is bigger		
Matches objects by colour		
Matches objects by shape		
Makes simple patterns with shapes		
Points to a named colour		
Points to a named shape		
Names five colours		
Names circle/square/triangle		
Selects own category to sort into (e.g. sorts animals into sheep/pigs, into sizes or into colours)		
Talks about shapes, describing and comparing		
Continues a given pattern with blocks/beads (e.g. red–yellow–red–yellow ...)		
Matches objects one-to-one (e.g. cups to saucers)		
Matches similar numbers (e.g. 2 to 2)		
Says which two sets have the 'same' number of objects in them		
Uses words like 'more' and 'less' when comparing		

Comments

Trackers   3–5

Area of Learning	Mathematical development
Play activity	Early counting

		✓	Date
Tries to count, sometimes in right order	👣		
Recognises sets of one, two or three objects	👣		
Joins in when you count steps			
Can show you 'five fingers'			
Says alternate number if you count '1 – 3 – 5'			
Counts out 1 to 3 from a larger set (e.g. give child six bricks and ask for three)			
Finds a grand total by counting two sets (e.g. adding a set of four bricks and three bricks)	👣		
Counts out five objects arranged in a line			
Spots errors when counting (e.g. '1, 2, 4 ... No! 1, 2, 3, 4')	👣		
Counts out six objects arranged randomly			
Joins in the counting in number rhymes (e.g. '1, 2, 3, 4, 5, once I caught a fish alive ...')			
Counts to 10 from memory	Ⓖ		
Counts out ten objects	Ⓖ		
Uses mathematical approaches for solving practical problems (e.g. 'If I have three cups, I need three saucers')	Ⓖ		
Begins to count beyond 10	👣		

Comments

Trackers 3–5

Area of Learning	Mathematical development
Play activity	Early number

		✓	Date
Enjoys number activities	👣		
Points to number representing their age	👣		
Uses marks or fingers to represent number	👣		
Says whether two numerals are the 'same' (e.g. matches card with '2' onto an identical card)			
Points to numerals to 3 when these are named			
Tries to write one or two numerals			
Uses numbers in talk (e.g. 'Danny had three')			
Traces over numerals			
Matches a numeral to a set of one to five (e.g. matches a card with '4' onto a group of four cars)	👣		
Points to numerals to 5 when these are named			
Begins to recognise numbers in the environment (e.g. notices and names a house number)			
Names numerals to 5	👣		
Can tell numerals from letters			
Names numerals 1 to 9	(G)		

Comments

Area of Learning

Physical development

Trackers 3–5

Area of Learning	Physical development
Play activity	Moving and balancing

		✓	Date
Runs fast out of doors			
Dances to music			
Finds three different ways of moving across a room (e.g. walking, jumping, crawling)	👣		
Moves in different ways to express feelings	👣		
Changes direction when running	👣		
Avoids obstacles when moving fast	👣		
Plays with different ways of moving and balancing (e.g. creeping, tiptoeing, bunny hopping along a bench)	👣		
Moves backwards and sideways as well as forwards	👣		
Marches to a steady rhythm			
Makes full and safe use of the climbing frame	👣		
Travels around/under/over/through equipment	👣		
Initiates new ideas for moving (e.g. when dancing)	👣		
Jumps from a ledge and lands safely	👣		
Moves with confidence and imagination (e.g. pretending to be a monster)	Ⓖ		
Moves with confidence and safety	Ⓖ		

Comments

Trackers 3–5

Area of Learning	Physical development
Play activity	Being active

	✓	Date
Plays actively out of doors		
Enjoys physical play		
Will join in a game of chase		
Understands the need to protect themselves in the sun		
Observes what changes when their body becomes active (e.g. feeling 'puffed', getting warm) 👣		
Understands why we need to sleep and rest 👣		
Manages to avoid collisions when playing active games 👣		
Can talk about 'healthy' food 👣		
Has a simple understanding of germs and staying clean		
Understands the need to drink plenty of liquid		
Knows that it is important to stay healthy Ⓖ		
Knows some of the things that help us to stay healthy Ⓖ		
Recognises body changes when they are active (e.g. heart rate, faster breathing) Ⓖ		
Shows awareness of space, of themselves and others Ⓖ		

Comments

Trackers   3–5

Area of Learning	Physical development
Play activity	Using tools

	✓	Date
Carefully handles and manipulates 'small world' objects such as farm animals, toy cars 👣		
Pats/pokes/squeezes/pinches/twists play doh 👣		
Uses simple tools with doh and materials 👣		
Cuts along a straight line with scissors		
Makes a simple construction with large materials (e.g. a model with packaging) 👣		
Uses a computer mouse to move a cursor		
Manipulates materials to achieve a planned effect (e.g. building a 'lorry') 👣		
Uses a computer mouse with a simple game		
Shows a clear preference for left/right hand 👣		
Cuts out a simple shape		
Takes some simple safety precautions without reminding (e.g. walks carefully when carrying scissors) 👣		
Handles malleable materials with increasing control (e.g. forms clay into sausages) Ⓖ		
Handles construction materials with increasing control (e.g. builds models from interlocking bricks) Ⓖ		
Handles tools and objects safely Ⓖ		
Uses a range of small and large equipment Ⓖ		

Comments

Area of Learning

Knowledge and understanding of the world

Trackers   3–5

Area of Learning	Knowledge and understanding of the world
Play activity	Finding out

		✓	Date
Talks about what is seen	👣		
Talks about what is happening	👣		
Looks inside/behind to see how things work			
Finds out what a seed needs in order to grow			
Notices and is interested in weather changes			
Asks questions about the natural world	👣		
Looks up information in a non-fiction picture book			
Notices and comments on patterns	👣		
Observes and finds out about where they live	G		
Finds out about their environment and talks about those features they like or dislike (e.g. 'I like my street because ...')	G		
Looks closely at similarities and differences (e.g. in different homes or towns)	G		
Looks closely at patterns and change (e.g. finds out what happens when a switch is operated on a simple circuit)	G		
Asks questions about how things work	G		
Asks questions about why things happen	G		

Comments

Trackers 3–5

Area of Learning	Knowledge and understanding of the world
Play activity	The world around us

		✓	Date
Describes simple objects	👣		
Describes simple events and experiences	👣		
Retells things that happened that were important to them	👣		
Shows an interest in the lives of familiar people (e.g. 'Where do you live?' 'Do you have a child too?')	👣		
Begins to differentiate between past and present (e.g. can tell you what happened when they were little)	👣		
Notices differences between features of the local environment (e.g. 'There's a new traffic light')	👣		
Examines objects and living things to find out more	👣		
Observes and finds out about the natural world	Ⓖ		
Finds out about past and present events in their own lives	Ⓖ		
Finds out about events in other people's lives	Ⓖ		
Uses their eyes, ears, touch and smell to investigate	Ⓖ		
Finds out about events they experience (e.g. 'Why do we need to go to the dentist?')	Ⓖ		
Finds out about some features of objects around them (e.g. asks what a smoke alarm is)	Ⓖ		
Finds out about some features of living things	Ⓖ		
Begins to know about their own culture and beliefs and those of other people	Ⓖ		

Comments

Trackers 3–5

Area of Learning	Knowledge and understanding of the world
Play activity	Construction

		✓	Date
Joins construction pieces together to build and balance	*f,*		
Begins to try out a range of tools safely (e.g. scissors, glue sticks, cleaning cloth)	*f,*		
Explores different techniques for constructing (e.g. glueing, stacking, interlocking)	*f,*		
Designs and makes a simple track layout with a toy train track			
Uses large cartons to construct a den			
Fits together interlocking construction bricks to make something			
Copies a simple design (e.g. a stairway of bricks)			
Can plan, construct and then review what has been made			
Can 'invent' something for a given purpose (e.g. a toy to keep a baby happy)			
Uses simple tools and techniques competently and appropriately	*f,*		
Selects the tools and techniques needed to shape, assemble and join materials they are using (e.g. when working with wood or cardboard)	Ⓖ		
Builds with a wide range of objects and resources (e.g. to make a den)	Ⓖ		
Adapts their work where necessary (e.g. to make it fit a certain space or do a certain job)	Ⓖ		

Comments

Trackers 3–5

Area of Learning	Knowledge and understanding of the world
Play activity	Early science and technology

	✓	Date
Shows an interest in computers 👣		
Takes part in a simple experiment (e.g. which things float/sink)		
Follows curiosity up with asking relevant questions		
Makes simple predictions in an experiment (e.g. 'what will happen if we let go of the balloon?'		
Can make simple generalisations (e.g. all full bottles are heavy)		
Can take part in a simple computer learning game 👣		
Shows an awareness of change (e.g. when we heat jelly it melts) 👣		
Finds out about everyday technology (e.g. knowing what a torch/radio/computer can be used for) Ⓖ		
Knows how to operate simple equipment such as a digital camera 👣		
Starts to use communication technology (e.g. a telephone) Ⓖ		
Can influence programmable equipment (e.g. makes a recording of their voice on CD) Ⓖ		
Can operate simple technology (e.g. cassette recorder/CD player)		

Comments

Area of Learning

Creative development

Trackers 3–5

Area of Learning	Creative development
Play activity	Just pretend

	✓	Date
Uses one object to represent another (e.g. 'This brush is my horse') 👣		
Uses available resources to create props (e.g. 'This box can be teddy's bed') 👣		
Puts a sequence of activities together to make a repertoire (e.g. making a cup of tea) 👣		
Acts out familiar routines with soft toys (e.g. having a tea party with the teddies)		
Enjoys stories based on themselves and familiar things 👣		
Plays alongside other children during imaginative play 👣		
Enjoys puppet play with another child		
Concentrates for ten minutes on transport play		
Introduces a storyline into their play (e.g. tells you they are going on a holiday) 👣		
Spends ten minutes happily engaged in the home/theme corner		
Plays cooperatively with others during imaginative play 👣		
Uses imagination in role play and pretend play Ⓖ		
Uses imagination in music and dance Ⓖ		
Uses imagination in art and design Ⓖ		

Comments

Trackers 3–5

Area of Learning	Creative development
Play activity	Music makers

		✓	Date
Shakes/bangs/scrapes a musical instrument			
Joins in with a few simple, familiar songs	👣		
Sings to themselves	👣		
Copies a simple rhythm by tapping/clapping	👣		
Dances confidently and freely			
Explores the different sounds of instruments	👣		
Plays loudly/softly in imitation			
Plays quickly/slowly in imitation			
Starts and stops playing an instrument when the background music starts or stops			
Sings and carries out actions at the same time (e.g. joining in 'Wheels on the bus' with words and actions)			
Responds to different music by moving in different ways (e.g. quickly or slowly)	Ⓖ		
Recognises and explores how sounds can be changed (e.g. playing loudly or softly)	Ⓖ		
Sings a simple song from memory	Ⓖ		
Continues a repeated sound pattern (e.g. continues a one-two rhythm when copying an adult)	Ⓖ		
Expresses their feelings using music/dance	Ⓖ		

Comments

Trackers   3–5

Area of Learning	Creative development
Play activity	Art and craft

	✓	Date
Paints a recognisable 'person'		
Explores what happens when they mix colours		
Experiments with mixing media (e.g. paint, glue, sand)		
Paints using several colours		
Paints a picture and describes it		
Draws a recognisable 'house'		
Uses grids, sun shapes and overlaps in ideas 👣		
Plans a creation ahead (e.g. 'I want to make a shiny blue sea picture') 👣		
Chooses colours to use for a purpose (e.g. fiery colours for the bonfire) 👣		
Talks about their creations 👣		
Uses art or craft to represent an experience (e.g. a holiday) 👣		
Experiments to create different textures (e.g. to make a rough or a smooth surface) 👣		
Paints a picture to represent what they feel (e.g. a 'happy' picture) Ⓖ		
Works creatively on a large scale (e.g. murals) 👣		
Explores colour and texture in two or three dimensions Ⓖ		

Comments

Trackers 3–5

Area of Learning	Creative development
Play activity	Materials

	✓	Date
Makes a simple collage by sticking pasta/feathers etc. to paper 👣		
Makes a simple 3-D construction with waste materials (e.g. a model out of boxes) 👣		
Further explores an experience using a range of senses or materials (e.g. how does it feel/look/smell/taste?) 👣		
Forms play doh into different shapes		
Describes experiences and past actions using a widening range of materials (e.g. acts out a past event with props) 👣		
Plans a construction ahead (e.g. 'I want to build a castle so I'll need ...') 👣		
Designs a model to a set idea (e.g. 'Can you make the giant's table?')		
Makes comparisons between materials using words like 'heavy', 'light', 'shiny', 'soft') 👣		
Selects the best materials for the job (e.g. to make a strong bridge)		
Designs a model that moves (e.g. one with wheels)		
Tries to capture experiences with materials (e.g. a sea collage with sand, shells and blue cellophane) 👣		
Knows which tools to use for different materials (e.g. in the woodworking corner)		
Expresses their feelings using designing and making (e.g. 'I like this because ...') Ⓖ		
Explores shape, form and space in 2-D or 3-D Ⓖ		

Comments

Appendix

Parent/Carer comments	Date

Contacts with outside agencies	Date